Pocketful of Miracles

Holiday Filefolder Games
Patterns and Directions

By Connie Eisenhart
and Ruth Bell

Appropriate for preschool, kindergarten, readiness and special education.
To motivate and reinforce beginning concepts.
Directions and patterns for individual or workshop contruction.

Written and Illustrated by
Connie Eisenhart
and Ruth Bell

Copyright © 1985

Published by
ℙℙ **PARTNER PRESS**
Box 124
Livonia, MI 48125

ISBN 0-933212-24-8

Distributed by:
 Gryphon House
3706 Otis Street
Mt. Rainer, Maryland 20822

PREFACE

If you are new to the concept of learning games being made and played on file folders you will soon discover the following:

- They are convenient to use and convenient to store.
- They fit well on tables and desks or are easily displayed to a group.
- They laminate well and come in bright attractive colors.
- Boxes that are designed to house file folders are an easy and inexpensive way to store your games.
- Boxes are readily available at discount drug stores or K-marts.
- Many games can be made from the same basic theme in varying levels of difficulty and a change of pattern.
- Reinforcement can be made more enjoyable and motivating.
- Stickers, wrapping paper, wall paper, coloring books or activity books are inexpensive resources for patterns or colorful pictures.
- You do not have to be particularly capable in art to produce a colorful and appealing, yet very individualized game.
- You can easily tailor a game to meet the specific needs of an individual group or child.
- The success of the games make them worth the time and effort to develop.

HELPFUL HINTS AND TIME SAVERS

1. Do laminate your game and game pieces. It enhances the colors and increases the life of the game.
2. Do reinforce your game pieces with tag board and recut them before laminating. Again, it increases the durability of the game and is well worth the extra effort. It is not mandatory, however. Clear contact paper is an alternative if you cannot laminate.
3. Do save patterns, extra wrapping paper or whatever in case you need to replace a playing piece.
4. Do staple a freezer weight Ziplock bag to the back of each game. This "Pocket" is an ideal way to store the game pieces.
5. Do lay your game out on the file folder before you glue it down so you will know things fit and what is the best arrangement.
6. Do any coloring before you cut out. That way you do not need to stay within lines and the coloring will go much faster.
7. Do any cutting of shadows or silhouettes at the same time as you cut the original. That not only assures exact matches but also reduces the amount of cutting. Cut double.
8. Do introduce the game to the children as a group even if your intention is to use the game as an independent activity. It eliminates repeating directions and assures that the children understand the object of the game and how it is to be played.
9. Do keep alert for ideas that can be adapted to this format and best meet the needs of your particular childen.
10. Don't use white glue straight from the bottle. It will leave ridges that show after being laminated. You can use a paint brush to spread the glue and that works satisfactorily. I prefer a glue stick or rubber cement. Rubber cement has the advantage that any excess can be rubbed off without damaging the game.
11. Don't laminate the game until the glue is completely dry.
12. Do leave a small margin when cutting little pictures rather than trying to cut every detail. It makes cutting so much easier.
13. Do enjoy the games with the children.

Good luck!

CONTENTS

Halloween

GAME: TRICK OR TREAT   COUNTING 1-1, NUMBER RECOGNITION

PURPOSE: To count 1-1 and identify the correct numeral.

HOW TO PLAY THE GAME: Match the number recorded on the back of each child to the corresponding amount of treats in each bag. Place the trick-or-treaters on the correct bag. For those ready for a visual discrimination challenge, the numbers are also hidden in the children's Halloween faces.

MATERIALS: patterns, scissors, markers, file folder, rubber cement, (tag board)

ASSEMBLY: Color and cut out the trick-or-treat bags and the Halloween trick-or-treaters. Mount the bags on the file folder. Mount the trick-or-treaters on tag board and recut. Print the numbers on the back of each child as follows: the clown 2, the devil 3, the witch 4, the Indian girl 5, the pirate 6, and the skeleton 7. Laminate and trim.

possible lay-out

bag patterns

bag patterns continued

JACK-O-LANTERNS   **VISUAL DISCRIMINATION**

PURPOSE: To match Jack-o-lanterns.

HOW TO PLAY THE GAME: Using the "right light" match the identical Jack-o-lanterns.

MATERIALS: game page, one 9 x 12 piece of construction paper, markers, aluminum foil, masking tape, rubber cement, paper punch

ASSEMBLY: Color the game page with markers. Mount it on a 9 x 12 piece of contstruction paper. Laminate and Trim. Paper punch holes next to each Jack-o-lantern. Wire the game sheet as illustrated on page 61.

Refer to Pages 59 - 62 for information on the "Right Light" and games to be played with the a continuity tester.

CONTINUITY TESTER

13

GAME: GHOST MATCH   **MATCHING IRREGULAR SHAPES AND FINGERPLAY PROP**

PURPOSE: To match ghosts to their silhouettes

HOW TO PLAY THE GAME: Have the children lay the ghosts on their matching silhouettes.

MATERIALS: lavender or other light colored construction paper, various markers, scissors, rubber cement, file folder, (tag board)

ASSEMBLY: By placing the lavender paper beneath the ghost patterns, cut 2 sets of ghosts. Color and cut out the remaining patterns. Mount white ghost game pieces on tag board and recut. Mount scene and lavender silhouettes on file folder. Laminate file folder, ghosts, and trim.

NOTE: This file folder may also be used to illustrate the fingerplay, "Five Little Jack-O-Lanterns Sitting on the Gate", Page 34 of **Finger Frolics,** Partner Press.

possible lay-out

Thanksgiving

GAME: SHIPS AHOY!   **DISCRIMINATING GRADUATED SIZES**

PURPOSE: To match ships graduated in size to their shadows. To reinforce counting 1-6.

HOW TO PLAY THE GAME: Have the children lay the ships on their shadows.

MATERIALS: black construction paper, scissors, rubber cement, markers, patterns, file folder, (tag board)

ASSEMBLY: Color the hulls of the ship patterns with 6 different markers. Color the masts black. By placing the black construction paper beneath the patterns, cut out the ship patterns and their shadows. Mount the colored ships on tag board and recut. Color and cut the rock pattern. Mount rock and shadows on file folder. Laminate and trim.

possible lay-out

GAME: FALL HARVEST   DEDUCTIVE REASONING, CONFIGUATION

PURPOSE: To complete the picture.

HOW TO PLAY THE GAME: Place the corresponding half of each picture next to its' counterpart to complete each picture.

MATERIALS: patterns, markers, file folder, scissors, rubber cement, (tag board)

ASSEMBLY: Mount the colored patterns on tag board. When the rubber cement is dry, cut out each pattern. Divide each pattern in two pieces. Mount half of each picture on the file folder. Trace around the other half to make the dotter line clue. Laminate file folder and pieces. Trim.

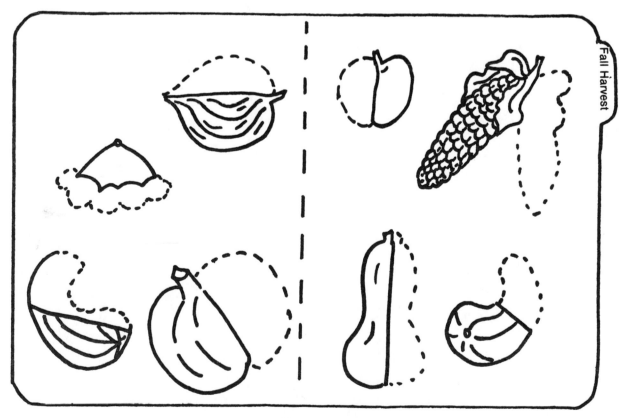

possible lay-out

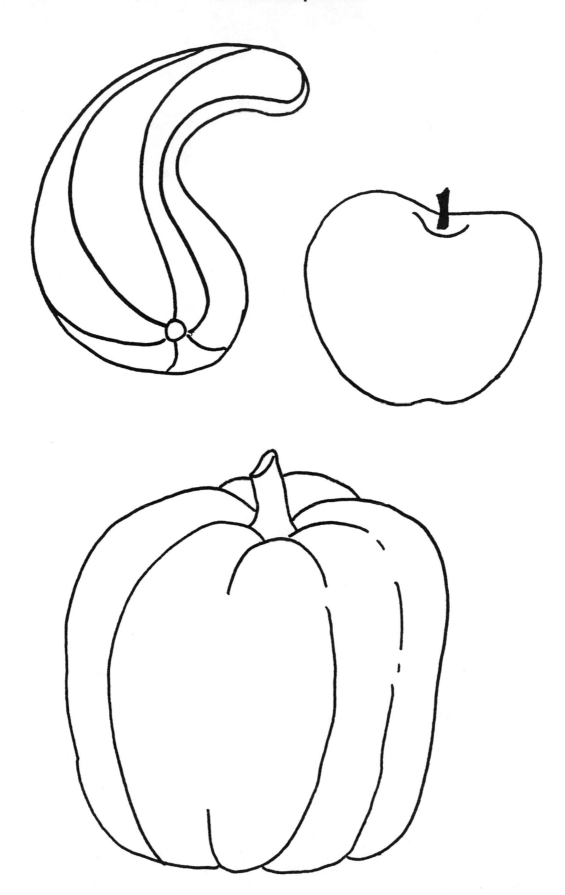

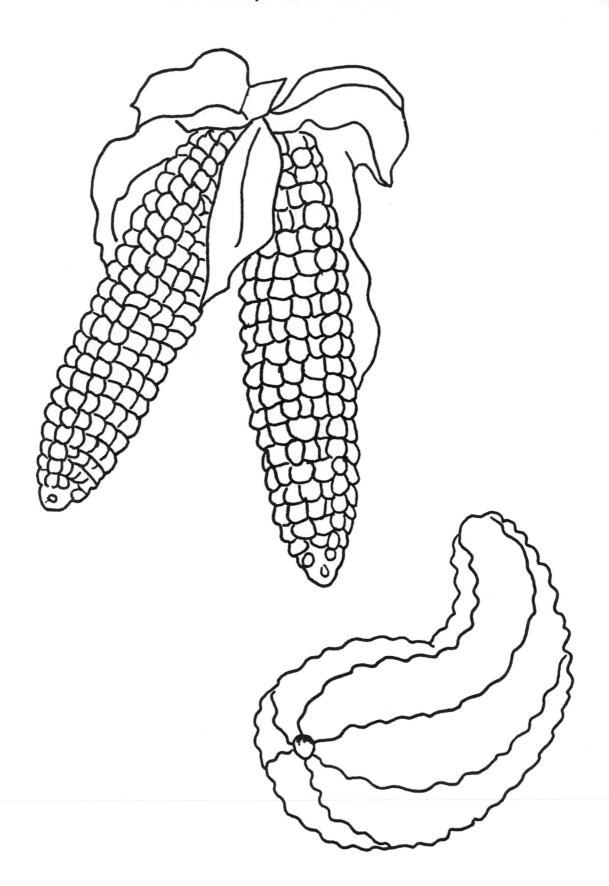

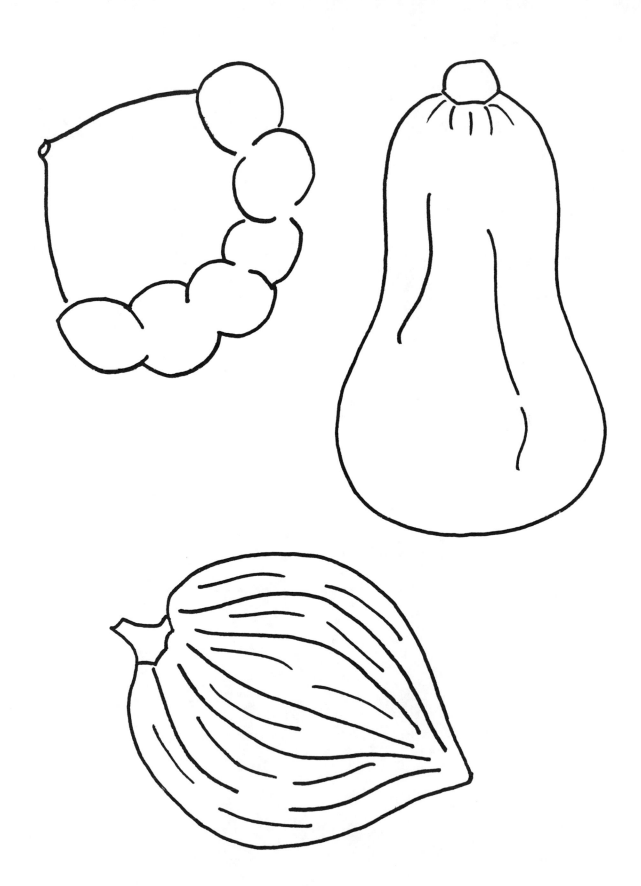

GAME: TURKEY FEATHERS   **REPEATING PATTERN**

PURPOSE: To put tail feathers on the turkey in the same sequence of colors as the turkey on the game board.

HOW TO PLAY THE GAME: The child inserts the feathers in the turkey to correspond with the gameboard. Naming the colors and counting the feathers can also be part of the activity.

MATERIALS: colored construction paper (9 colors for 7 different feathers, body, and feet), scissors, rubber cement, fine black marker, file folder, (tag board)

ASSEMBLY: Cut 2 sets of pattern pieces, using 7 different colors for the feathers. Mount complete turkey on the left side of file folder as suggested on layout, On the right side mount the body, head, and feet. On the body, glue only the edges. DO NOT GLUE THE TOP PART OF THE BODY (as indicated on the pattern). Mount one set of feathers on tag board. Cut out. Laminate and trim. With a razor blade carefully slit the laminating film on the top edge of the body. This forms the slot to insert the feathers.

possible lay-out

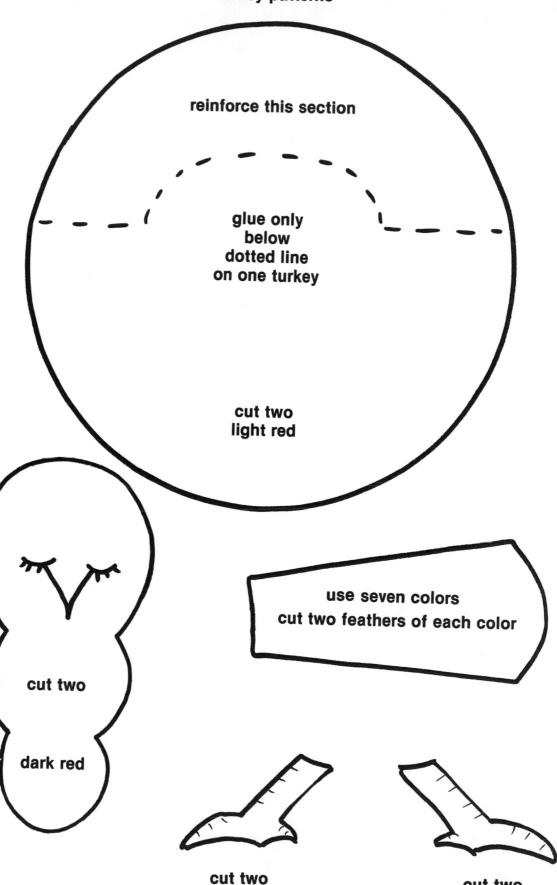

reinforce this section

glue only
below
dotted line
on one turkey

cut two
light red

cut two

dark red

use seven colors
cut two feathers of each color

cut two

cut two

Christmas

GAME: HOLIDAY BULBS   **VISUAL DISCRIMINATION**

PURPOSE: To match holiday tree bulbs

HOW TO PLAY THE GAME: Using the "right light" match the identical bulbs.

MATERIALS: game page, one 9 x 12 piece of construction paper, markers, aluminum foil, masking tape, rubber cement, paper punch and/or paper drill.

ASSEMBLY: Color the game sheet with markers. Mount it on a 9 x 12 piece or construction paper. Laminate and trim. Paper punch or drill holes next to each bulb. Wire the game sheet as illustrated on page 61.

NOTE: If you do not have a paper drill the inside holes can be punched by creasing the paper slightly and punching only half of the circle on the fold. Do this for each hole. The game sheet can be flattened again by ironing with a **warm** iron.

Refer to Pages 59 - 62 for information on the "Right Light" and games to be played with a continuity tester.

CONTINUITY TESTER

GAME: COOKIE JAR

PURPOSE: To recognize numbers and count 1-1.

HOW TO PLAY THE GAME: Count and place the correct number of cookies in each cookie jar.

MATERIALS: patterns, scissors, markers, construction paper in your choice of colors, rubber cement, file folder, holiday stickers

ASSEMBLY: Using patterns cut cookie jars from construction paper and mount them on file folder. Glue the jar lid down completely but glue only the sides and bottom of the jar itself. This will form a pocket. Decorate the jars with stickers and add the numbers. Cut from construction paper the number and kind of cookies you will need. Use markers to add details. Laminate and trim the file folder and cookies. Using a razor blade carefully slit the laminating film along the top edge of the jar. Be careful not to cut the file folder itself. In this way the cookies can be placed inside the jar (pocket) as the game is played.

possible lay-out

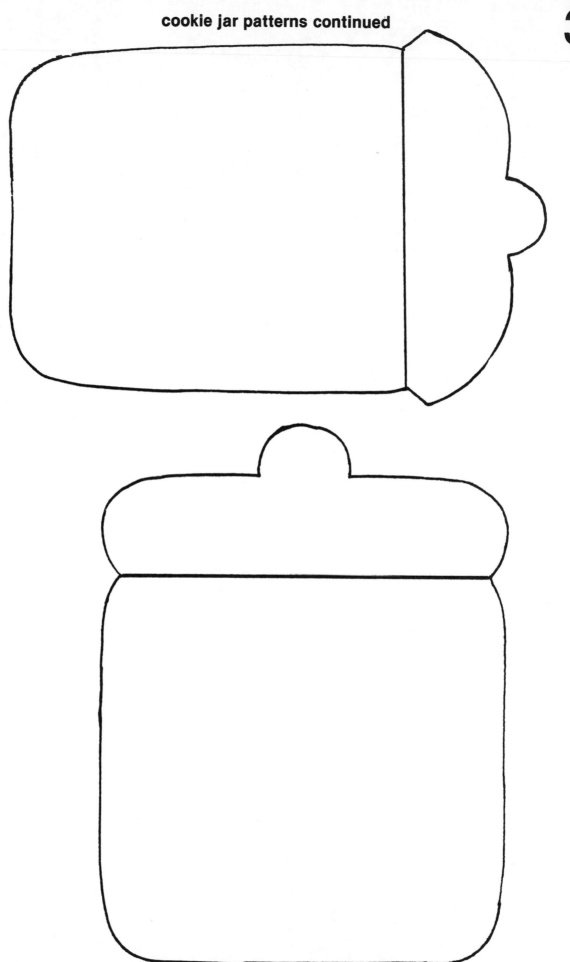

GAME: HOLIDAY GIFTS

PURPOSE: To determine the appropriate size gift box for each toy.

HOW TO PLAY THE GAME: Place the proper size gift boxes on the appropriate toy.

MATERIALS: patterns, markers, scissors, file folder, rubber cement, (tag board)

ASSEMBLY: Color the patterns and cut them all out. Mount the toys on the file folder. Mount the gift boxes on tag board and recut. Laminate and trim.

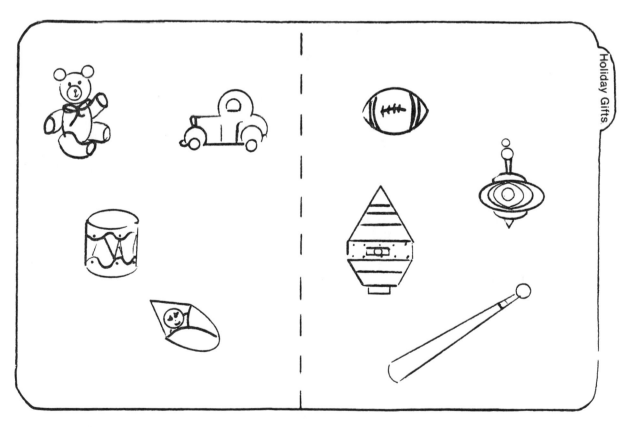

possible lay-out

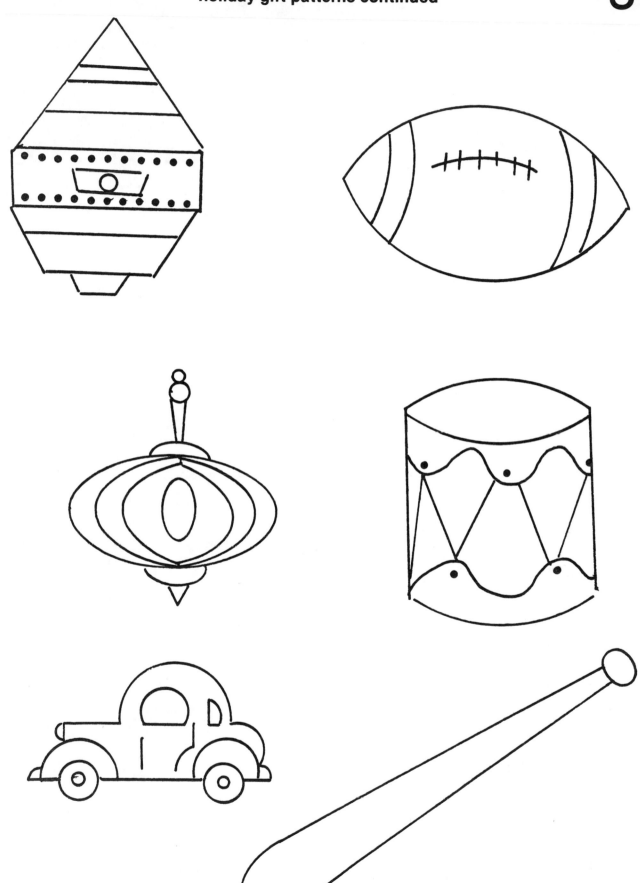

Valentines

GAME: HEARTS GALORE   WHICH ONE DOESN'T BELONG?

PURPOSE: To find the heart that is different in each line.

HOW TO PLAY THE GAME: Have the children look at the 3 hearts in each line. Cover the one that is different with a 2 inch square of paper.

MATERIALS: various red and pink markers, scissors, rubber cement, file folder. (I like red or pink for this game.)

ASSEMBLY: Color the hearts red, white, and pink. Make sure that the matching hearts on each line are colored exactly the same. Cut out hearts and mount on file folder as shown on lay-out sheet. If you do not wish to cut out the hearts (to conserve time and effort), the entire lay-out sheet may be mounted on a file folder. Laminate and trim.

GAME: COMPLETE THE VALENTINE   **PATTERN MATCHING**

PURPOSE: To complete the valentine by finding matching pieces.

HOW TO PLAY THE GAME: Have the children lay the matching valentine half next to it's mate on the game board.

MATERIALS: valentine patterns, white construction paper, a variety of red, white, and pink wrapping paper, scissors, rubber cement, (pink) file folder, (tag board)

ASSEMBLY: Cut 2 sets of each valentine at the same time, one of white construction paper and one of wrapping paper. Mount the white set on the file folder. Mount the left half of the wrapping paper hearts on the white heart of the same size. Mount the right half on tag board. Cut out. Laminate and trim.

possible lay-out

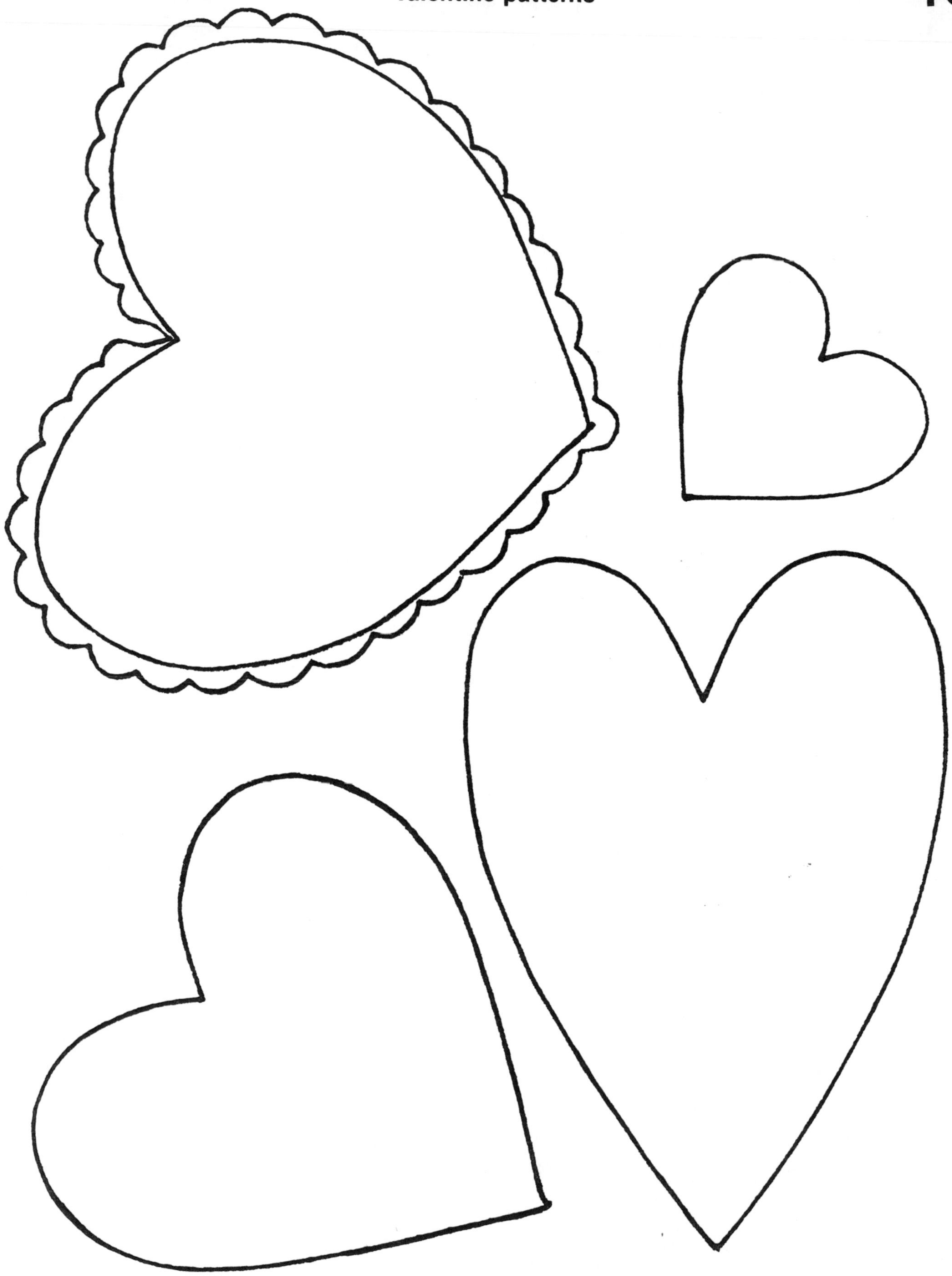

GAME: LOADS OF VALENTINES   **S,M,L FIGURE GROUNDING**

PURPOSE: To find, count, and match hearts of three sizes.

HOW TO PLAY THE GAME: Match all the white hearts to the exact size hearts on the file folder. When used as a group activity or with teacher direction, count each size heart.

MATERIALS: white construction paper, rubber cement, scissors, red file folder, (tag board)

ASSEMBLY: Cut out patterns cutting 10 small hearts, 8 medium hearts, and 6 large hearts. Mount 5 small, 4 medium, and 3 large white hearts on the file folder as indicated or use a design that pleases you. They may overlap or not as you desire for your group. Overlapping increases the difficulty of the game. Glue the remaining hearts on tag board and re-cut. Laminate and trim.

VARIATION: You might enjoy making a second set of game pieces in three colors or even many colors to extend the activity.

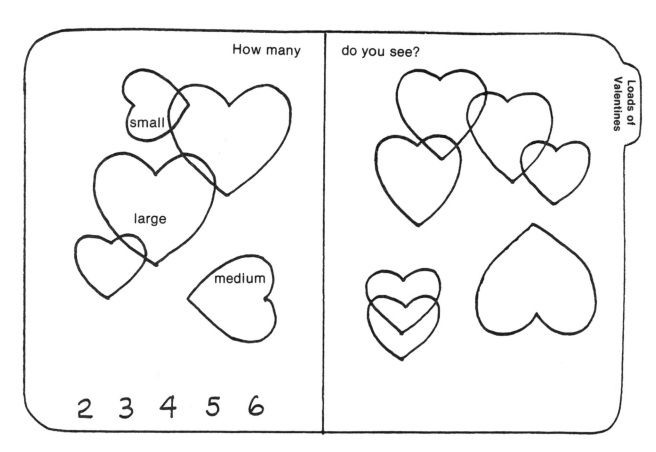

possible lay-out

cut 6 white
cut 3 pink

cut 8 white
cut 4 lavender

cut 10 white
cut 5 blue

2 3 4 5 6

Easter

GAME: HATCHING DUCKLINGS   **MATCHING NUMERALS**

PURPOSE: To match numerals.

HOW TO PLAY THE GAME: Place the duckling in the shell with the corresponding numerals.

MATERIALS: scissors, patterns, markers, yellow and white construction paper, file folder, rubber cement, clear contact paper, (tag board)

ASSEMBLY: Cut eight yellow ducks and eight white shells. Add features and numbers with markers. Mount the shells and ducklings on tag board and re-cut. Laminate the file folder, shells and ducklings. Trim. Mount the egg shells on the file folder using clear contact paper squares. Leave the jagged edge open so it forms a pocket for the duckling to slip into.

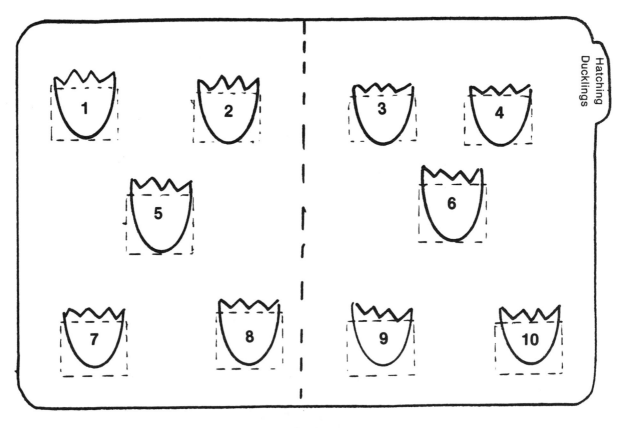

possible lay-out

GAME: DRESS THE BUNNY   **DUPLICATING PATTERNS**

PURPOSE: To duplicate the exact clothing arrangement using a visual clue.

HOW TO PLAY THE GAME: Put the rabbit card of your choice in the pocket to use as a guide. Selecting from the clothing assortment, dress the rabbit as the card illustrates.

MATERIALS: rabbit cards provided, large rabbit and clothing patterns, eight xerox copies of clothing patterns to color *or* various colors of construction paper to cut out clothing, markers, scissors, rubber cement, tape, file folder, (tag board)

ASSEMBLY: Using markers color the large rabbit's features and the outfits of the rabbit on the cards. Color the clothing patterns to match the cards (or cut them from colored paper if that was your choice). Cut out the large rabbit and mount it on one side of the file folder. Cut out the cards, mount them on tag board and recut them. Also cut out the pieces of clothing. Laminate the file folder, cards and clothing. Trim. Tape two pieces of laminating film (cut from scraps) to form pockets in which clothing may be stored and card selection may be displayed for reference.

possible lay-out

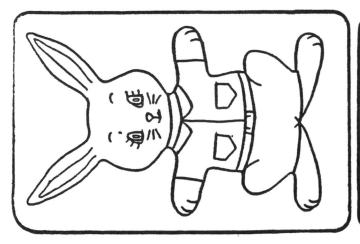
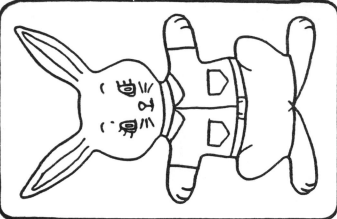
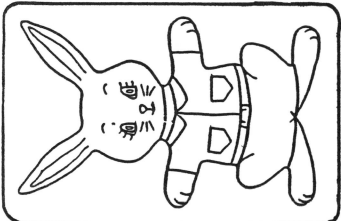
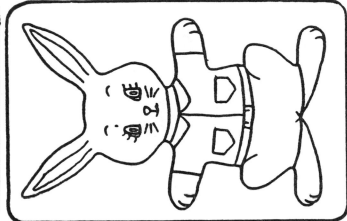
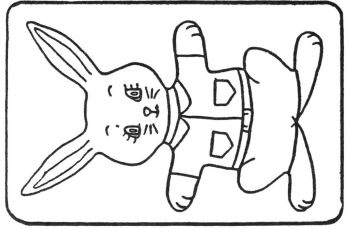
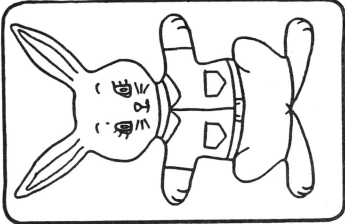
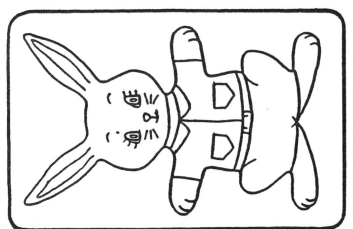
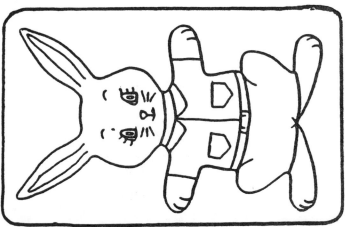

GAME: EGG MATCH   **COMPLETE THE PICTURE**

PURPOSE: To match puzzle edges.

HOW TO PLAY THE GAME: Complete the egg shapes by matching the puzzle edges and placing each so it appears to interlock and makes it whole.

MATERIALS: various colored construction paper, egg patterns, scissors, rubber cement, file folder, (tag board)

ASSEMBLY: Cut out the egg patterns. Cut them in half as patterns indicate. Cut each half of a different colored construction paper. (This assures the children will match edges not colors). Mount one-half of each egg on the file folder. Mount the other half on tag board and recut. Laminate file folder and game pieces. Trim.

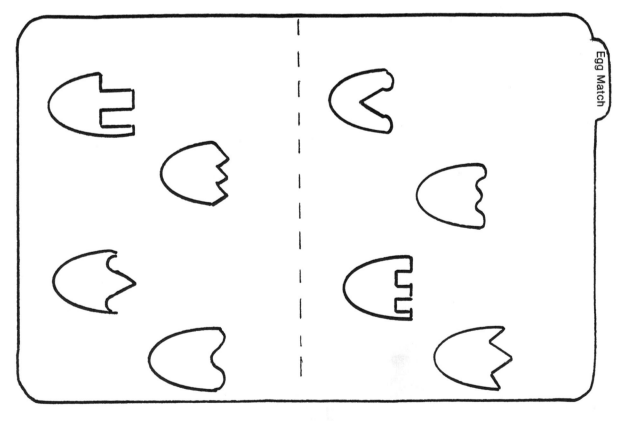

possible lay-out

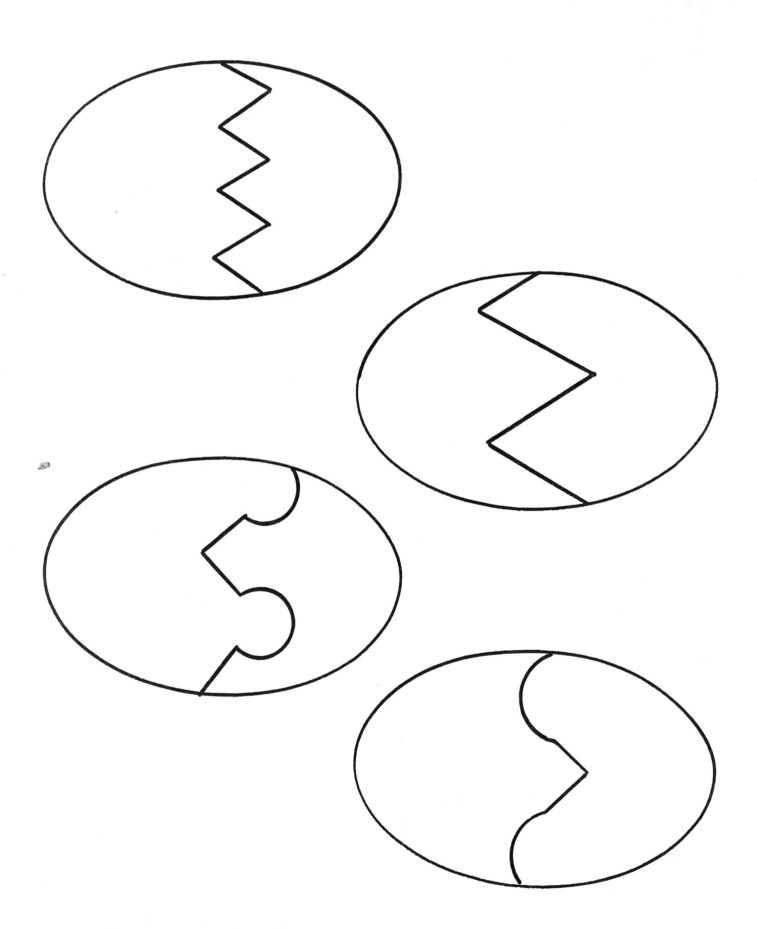

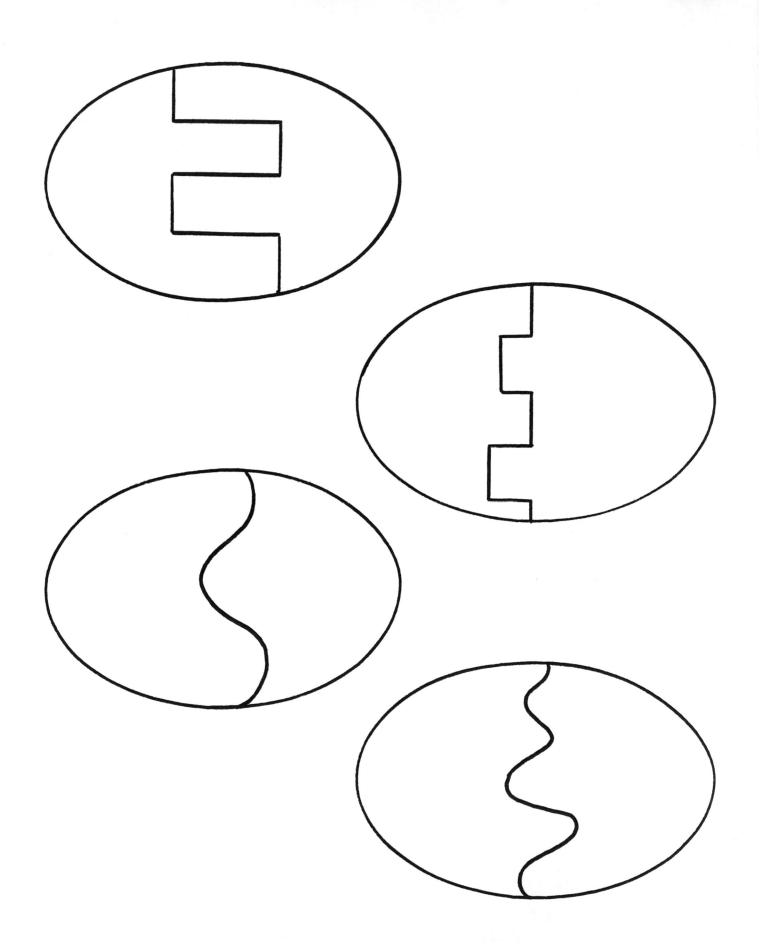

Right
Light

**continuity
tester
games**

GENERAL INFORMATION FOR ALL "RIGHT LIGHT" GAMES

GAME: THE "RIGHT LIGHT"   **SKILL OF YOUR CHOICE**

PURPOSE: To light up the "Right Light" by touching two answers that go together.

INTRODUCE THE GAME: Before the game is played it must be introduced to the group so they become aware of how the tool is used and what it can do. Explain to the children that: this game uses a tool called a continuity tester. It has batteries inside that give it electricity. When the two ends of the tester touch things that are wired together in certain ways, the electricity will travel in a circle and make the light shine. This game can do this. Aluminium foil is used to wire it. It's taped on the back. (Show them.) Beside each picture is a dot where the wire (foil) shows through. (Show them.) By looking at all the things in the first row we can see they go together (match) with things in the other row. If you touch the ends of the continuity tester to the dots of two things that go together, it will light up! (Show them.) It will not light if we touch dots beside pictures of things that do not go together. (Show them.) It only lights when you are right. You do not need to open the end of the continuity tester or press hard. A gentle touch will do but **both** ends must be touching the foil dots.

THIS MIGHT NOT BE APPROPRIATE FOR ALL GROUPS. MEET THE NEEDS OF YOUR GROUP BUT DO BRIEF THEM ON THE ESSENTIAL FACTS.

CONTINUITY TESTERS ARE AVAILABLE IN MOST HARDWARE STORES IN THE ELECTRICAL OR AUTOMOTIVE DEPARTMENT. THEY RANGE IN PRICE FROM $1.85 TO $6.00. THEY ALL SEEM TO WORK WELL. SOMETIMES THEY COME WITH AN EXTENDED POINT THAT CAN BE DANGEROUS TO CHILDREN. THE POINT CAN EASILY BE SNIPPED OF WITH WIRE CUTTERS AT ½" AND SANDED SMOOTH WITH SANDPAPER. ALL TESTERS USE BATTERIES. I HAVE FOUND THE MORE EXPENSIVE MODEL VERY WELL CONSTRUCTED BUT CUMBERSOME FOR LITTLE HANDS TO USE COMFORTABLY. I USE THE LESS EXPENSIVE MODEL.

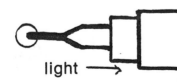

light →

CONTINUITY TESTER

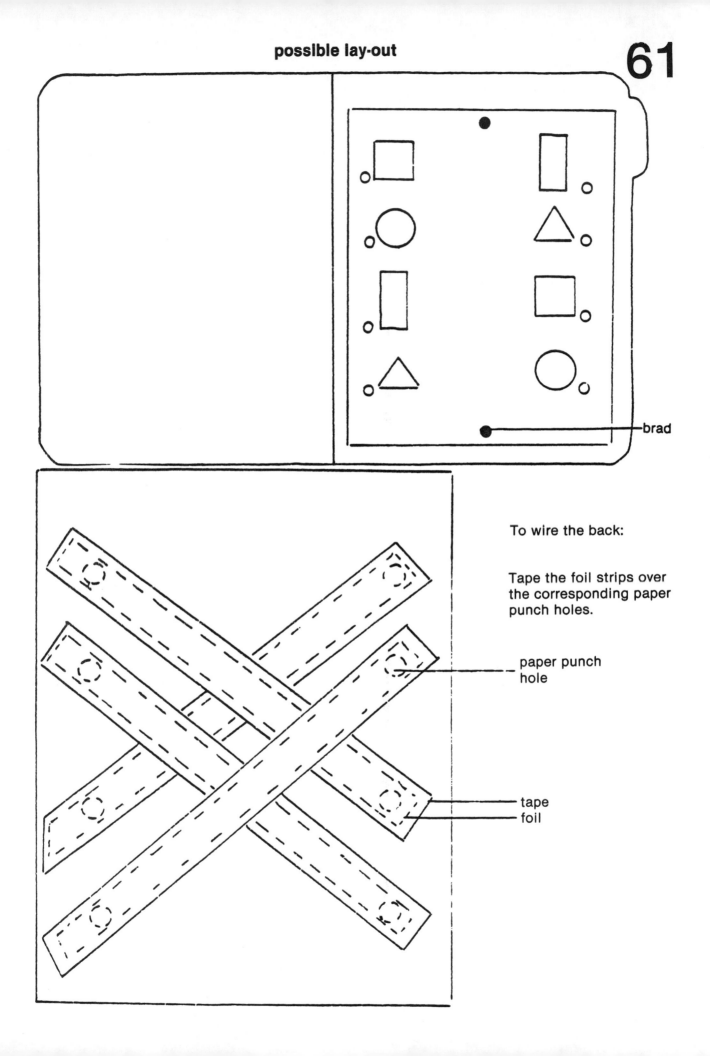

brad

To wire the back:

Tape the foil strips over the corresponding paper punch holes.

paper punch hole

tape

foil

62

GAME: JACK-O-LANTERNS
HOLIDAY BULBS

A SELF CHECKING TOOL FOR
MOTIVATING LEARNING AND
INDEPENDENT REINFORCEMENT.

PURPOSE: To make a correct connection and, therefore, light up the "right light".

HOW TO PLAY THE GAME: Find the corresponding answers and place each end of the "right light" on the appropriate dots. If a correct match has been made, it will light up.

MATERIALS: a game sheet that has been colored, mounted on a 9 x 12 piece of construction paper, laminated, trimmed and punched with holes. (See illustration), masking tape and aluminum foil

ASSEMBLY: Fold a 2 inch strip of foil to a ½ inch width giving you 3-4 thicknesses. On the back of the game sheet tape the foil to the holes of matching sets of pictures. (See illustration). Tape each strip individually, being sure each is completely covered with tape before doing the next. (If the foil of one touches the foil of another, it will conduct the electricity to the wrong answers as well as the right ones). Continue until the entire game sheet is wired. Test it out.

NOTE: After being wired, if you wish, the game sheet can be attached to a laminated file folder using brads at the top and bottom of the game sheet. This eliminates accidental damage to the wiring. The game sheet can easily be inter-changed as skill and seasons change.

LOOK FOR:
Pocketful of Miracles Set I, file folder games
Pocketful of Miracles, patterns and activities
Pocketful of Miracles Set II, file folder games